Sharks /
J597.3 Lop   144500

Lopez, Gary.
Wilton Public Library

SHARKS

by Gary Lopez

The Child's World®

Content Adviser:
Jonathan Bird,
President, Oceanic
Research Group, Inc.

Published in the United States of America by The Child's World®
PO Box 326 • Chanhassen, MN 55317-0326
800-599-READ • www.childsworld.com

PHOTO CREDITS
© Amos Nachoum/Corbis: 8, 18
Animals Animals © Bob Cranston: 19
© Brandon D. Cole: cover, 6-7, 14, 17, 23
© Comstock, 2
© David Nardini/Getty: 13
© Georgette Douwma/Getty: 4-5
© Jeffrey L. Rotman/Corbis: 9
© Jeff Rotman/Jeff Rotman Photography: 25, 27
© Koji Nakamura/Jeff Rotman Photography: 20-21
© Michael Prince/Corbis: 29
© PhotoDisc: 3, 31
© Richard Herrmann/Getty: 10-11

ACKNOWLEDGMENTS
The Child's World®: Mary Berendes, Publishing Director;
Katherine Stevenson, Editor

The Design Lab: Kathleen Petelinsek, Design and Page Production

LIBRARY OF CONGRESS CATALOGING-IN-PUBLICATION DATA
Lopez, Gary.
  Sharks / by Gary Lopez.
      p. cm. — (New naturebooks)
  Includes bibliographical references and index.
  ISBN 1-59296-649-7 (library bound : alk. paper)
  1. Sharks—Juvenile literature. I. Title. II. Series.
  QL638.9.L63 2006
  597.3—dc22   2005033838

Table of Contents

4 Meet the Shark!

6 What Do Sharks Look Like?

10 Are There Different Kinds of Sharks?

12 Are Sharks Dangerous?

16 How Do Sharks Hunt?

20 What Are Baby Sharks Like?

22 Are Sharks Important?

24 Do Sharks Have Enemies?

26 Can We Learn More About Sharks?

30 *Glossary*

31 *To Find Out More*

32 *Index*

On the cover: You can see the rows of sharp teeth in this great white shark's mouth.

Meet the Shark!

Scientists believe sharks have been around for about 400 million years.

Megalodon **was a huge, meat-eating shark that lived as recently as 1.7 million years ago. Its teeth were as big as an adult human hand!**

The ocean water is clear and blue in the bright sunshine. Under the surface, schools of colorful fish swim through the water. Among them swims a sleek animal with a long tail and very sharp teeth. This animal is cruising through the water looking for its next meal. People all over the world fear this creature. What is it? It's a shark!

This silky shark is surrounded by fish called anthias. Silky sharks get their name from their skin, which appears smoother than the skin of other sharks.

What Do Sharks Look Like?

Sharks do not have bones in their bodies. Instead, their skeletons are made up of a bendable material called cartilage.

Sharks' tails are uneven—the upper half is always longer than the lower half.

Like all fish, sharks have long, rounded bodies and powerful tails. On their sides, sharks have two **fins** that help them change directions as they swim. On the sides of their heads, sharks have a number of slits called **gills**. The sharks use their gills to breathe.

Sharks have very rough skin. In fact, many people say that it feels like sandpaper. A shark's skin is rough because it is made up of thousands of **dermal denticles**. These are tiny, scale-like plates that overlap each other.

From close up, you can see the rough skin of this epaulette shark. Epaulette sharks live in the warm, shallow waters around Australia and New Guinea.

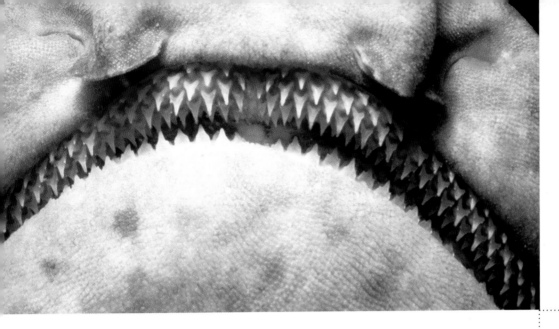

A close-up view of this California swell shark's mouth shows rows and rows of teeth.

Most sharks also have dozens of sharp teeth. These teeth help the sharks hold on to the slippery foods they eat. A shark's teeth keep growing as long as the shark is alive. When one tooth breaks or falls out, another grows in its place.

Whale sharks and basking sharks are huge animals. They have hundreds of teeth, but they are very tiny. That's because these sharks don't use their teeth for feeding. Instead, they eat by simply opening their large mouths and swimming slowly through the water. Tiny animals such as shrimp, krill, and **plankton** wash in and get trapped in small filters in the shark's gills.

Some kinds of sharks lose as many as 30,000 teeth during their lifetime.

This whale shark is about 40 feet (12 meters) long. The fish swimming in front of its mouth are also feeding on plankton. These little fish swim just far enough ahead of the shark to avoid being swallowed by mistake.

Are There Different Kinds of Sharks?

Collared carpetsharks can change color to match the ocean floor where they rest and feed.

Shortfin mako sharks are thought to be one of the fastest fishes in the ocean. They can swim as fast as 60 mph (97 kph).

There are more than 450 different **species** of sharks. Some sharks, such as mako sharks and tiger sharks, can grow to be fairly large. Most sharks, however, are small. In fact, half of all shark species are shorter than a baseball bat! Many of these small sharks live on the seafloor in shallow water. They eat creatures such as shrimp and worms buried in the sand.

This female shortfin mako shark is swimming just off the California coast. Makos feed mostly on fish called mackerel.

10

Are Sharks Dangerous?

Great whites grow about 10 inches (25 cm) per year and can go as long as three months without eating.

Female great whites are usually larger than males.

Great whites sometimes stick their heads out of the water to look around.

Smaller sharks are fairly gentle animals. Even many of the larger types are harmless. But some types of sharks can be dangerous. The great white shark is one shark that should be left alone. It can grow to be 20 feet (6 m) long and weigh almost 3,000 pounds (1,361 kg)! It has very powerful jaws and hundreds of sharp teeth. Great white sharks eat bigger animals such as seals, sea lions, and dolphins.

This huge great white shark is swimming just off the coast of Guadalupe Island, Mexico. To take this picture safely, the photographer stayed in an underwater cage made of metal.

Sharks are most dangerous when they are hungry, bothered, or scared. When they are hungry or upset, sharks sometimes attack people. Many shark attacks probably happen when sharks mistake people for one of their usual foods. Unlike the way they're shown in scary movies, sharks don't set out to hunt people. Most of the time, they stay far away from people.

When a shark becomes aggressive, it arches its back and points its front fins downward.

Worldwide, fewer than 100 people are attacked by sharks each year.

These bull sharks are swimming near a beach in the Bahamas. Bull sharks are one of the types most likely to attack people. That's because they live and feed in shallow waters where people swim and play.

How Do Sharks Hunt?

Sharks can smell their prey from about 1 mile (1.6 km) away.

Sharks use their nostrils only for smelling—they never use them for breathing as we do.

Some sharks can detect just one drop of blood in 25 gallons (95 liters) of water.

Sharks find their food by using all their senses. They use their keen sense of smell to find food that is far away. Tiny movements, or **vibrations**, in the water let them know right where the animal is. As they get closer, the sharks smell and taste the "flavor" of the animal in the water. They also see their victim, or **prey**, as it swims along.

Sharks have one last trick to help them find their prey—they can sense electricity! All living things give off tiny amounts of electricity. So if a shark's senses of sight and smell don't lead it to its prey, sensing the electricity in the water often does. Little holes called **pores** on the shark's snout lead to special organs that detect tiny amounts of electricity, guiding the shark toward its meal.

Like all sharks, this tiger shark uses its nostrils to smell. This picture also shows the small pores that help the shark sense electricity.

This blue shark is eating a mackerel off the California coast. Blue sharks are fast swimmers and often hunt fast-moving prey.

Small and big sharks have different ways of catching their prey. Small sharks slowly sneak up on their prey and then quickly gulp it down. Bigger sharks must work harder for their meals. When a big shark is ready to eat, it circles around its prey. It must be careful not to scare the animal. When it is close enough, the shark swims under the animal and quickly attacks it, biting down with its sharp teeth.

Thresher sharks use their long, whiplike tails to stun and frighten fish into a group, where they are easier to catch.

You can see straight down into the mouth of this great white shark. It's about to attack the metal cage the photographer is swimming in to keep safe.

What Are Baby Sharks Like?

Baby sharks are born with a full set of teeth.

Depending on the species, sharks produce between 2 and 135 pups at a time.

Shark egg cases are sometimes called "mermaids' purses" because of their strange and beautiful shapes.

Different kinds of sharks have their babies, or *pups,* in different ways. Most sharks give birth to live young that can swim just as soon as they are born. Others lay eggs that attach to rocks and weeds. From the moment they hatch or are born, shark pups must live on their own. They learn to eat and stay safe all by themselves. Like most other animals, shark pups look just like their parents, only smaller.

20

This baby catshark is just breaking out of its egg case. Catsharks get their name from their long, catlike eyes, which glow when a light is shined into them.

Are Sharks Important?

Hammerhead sharks swing their heads from side to side as they swim. Scientists think this movement helps the sharks smell their prey.

Sharks are very important animals. By eating other animals, sharks help keep the oceans healthy. They eat weak or sick animals, leaving the healthy ones more room to eat and live. Without sharks and other **predators**, our oceans would be overflowing with animals, and many of them would be sick.

This great hammerhead shark is swimming in warm waters near the Bahamas. You can see how hammerheads got their name—their head is shaped much like a hammer. There are several different species of hammerheads, but the great hammerhead is the largest.

Do Sharks Have Enemies?

The longest-living shark species is the spiny dogfish, which can live for 100 years.

Sharks have few natural enemies in their ocean world. In fact, sharks' biggest enemy is people. People throughout the world kill sharks to eat or sell their meat and fins. Some people who fish for a living kill sharks because they eat other fish. Sharks also die when they get caught in fishing nets by mistake.

24

A diver checks this dead sand tiger shark that was caught in an anti-shark net. The net was set to keep sharks away from a beach in South Africa.

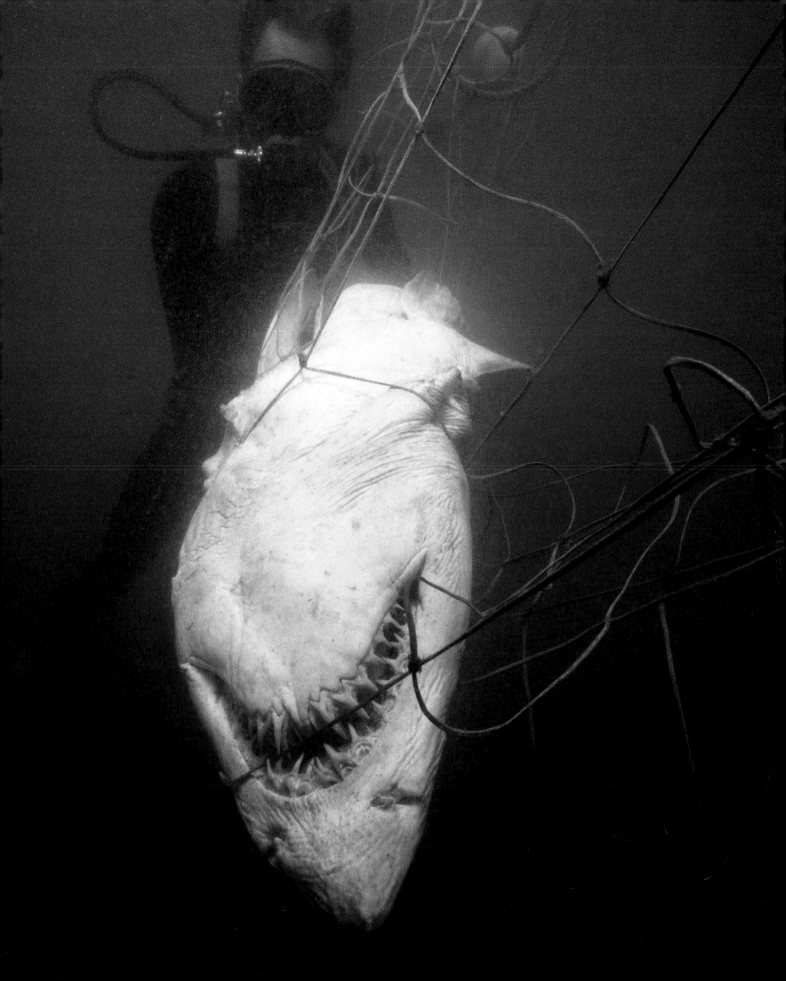

Can We Learn More About Sharks?

Sharks rarely get cancer. Scientists are studying them to learn more about curing this disease in humans.

Although we have learned a lot about sharks, there is still a lot we do not know. Some types of sharks swim in very deep water, and we know very little about how they live. Scientists still have questions even about the sharks we see all the time. To answer these questions, the scientists are studying all they can about sharks. They learn from sharks kept in zoos. They also learn about sharks by swimming with them—with lots of safety equipment, of course!

These scientists are putting a tiny tracking device inside a young scalloped hammerhead. The gray tube helps them place the device safely in the shark's stomach. After the shark is back in the water, computers track where it goes. The scientists don't have much time to study it, though—after a few days, the shark spits up the device and leaves it behind.

Sharks must keep moving, at least a little, or they tend to sink.

When turned upside down, sharks fall into a kind of "sleep" where they are very relaxed. This "sleep" is called *tonic immobility.*

Sharks are some of nature's most interesting animals. Sadly, they are also misunderstood. Instead of learning more about sharks, many people are simply afraid of them. But for anyone interested in sharks, there are still plenty of mysteries to be solved!

Going to an aquarium where you can see sharks up close is a great way to learn more about them!

Glossary

cartilage (KAR-tuh-lij) Cartilage is a bendable material that makes up certain body parts in animals and humans. Instead of bones, a shark's skeleton is made of cartilage.

dermal denticles (DER-mul DENT-ik-ulz) A shark's skin is made up of thousands of dermal denticles. The denticles are tiny, scale-like plates that overlap each other.

fins (FINZ) Fins are the flaps on a fish's body that help it change directions as it swims. A shark has fins on the top and sides of its body.

gills (GILZ) Sharks breathe through thin slits called gills. As water passes over the gills, air gets trapped and enters the shark's body.

plankton (PLANK-tun) Plankton are very tiny animals and plants that live in the ocean. Some sharks eat plankton.

pores (PORZ) Pores are tiny holes in a person's or animal's skin. Sharks' pores help them detect electricity in the water.

predators (PRED-uh-turz) Predators are animals that hunt and kill other animals. Sharks are predators.

prey (PRAY) Prey animals are hunted and eaten by other animals. Many sea creatures are prey for sharks.

species (SPEE-sheez) A species is a different type of a certain animal. There are more than 450 different species of sharks.

vibrations (vy-BRAY-shunz) Vibrations are tiny movements. Sharks hunt by sensing vibrations in the water.

To Find Out More

Watch it!

National Geographic Society. *Shark Encounters.* VHS. Burbank, CA: Columbia TriStar Home Video, 1991.

Sharks: Two Complete Programs: Great White & The Ultimate Guide to Sharks. DVD. Santa Monica, CA: Discovery Channel Video, 2001.

Read it!

Arnosky, Jim. *All About Sharks.* New York: Scholastic, 2003.

Berger, Melvin, Gilda Berger, and John Rice (illustrator). *What Do Sharks Eat for Dinner?: Questions and Answers About Sharks.* New York: Scholastic Reference, 2001.

Bird, Jonathan. *Adventures with Sharks.* Flagstaff, AZ.: Best Publishing, 2003.

Llewellyn, Claire. *The Best Book of Sharks.* Boston: Kingfisher, 2005.

Mallory, Kenneth. *Swimming with Hammerhead Sharks.* Boston: Houghton Mifflin, 2001.

Troll, Ray. *Sharkabet: A Sea of Sharks from A to Z.* Portland, OR.: WestWinds Press, 2002.

On the Web

Visit our home page for lots of links about sharks:
http://www.childsworld.com/links

Note to Parents, Teachers, and Librarians: We routinely check our Web links to make sure they're safe, active sites—so encourage your readers to check them out!

31

Index

About the Author

Gary Lopez, PhD, studied marine biology at Scripps Institution of Oceanography. After teaching at the University of California, San Diego, Gary produced and directed documentary films for Encyclopaedia Britannica, PBS, and The Cousteau Society (Jacques Cousteau). Today, Gary is still producing television documentaries and is also the Executive Director of the Monterey Institute for Technology and Education, which provides online courses to students all over the world.

Appearance, 4, 6, 10
attacks by, 15, *15*

Basking shark, 9
blue shark, 19
bull shark, *15*

California swell shark, 9
cancer in, *26*
cartilage, 6
catshark, *20*
collared carpetshark, *10*

Dangers of, 12
dermal denticles, 6

Eggs, 20, *20*
enemies, 24
epaulette shark, 6

Feeding, 9, 19
filters, 9
fins, 6, *15*
food. *See* prey.

Gills, 6
great white shark, 12, *12*, 19

Hammerhead shark, *22*
hunting, 4, 16, 19, *22*

Importance of, 22

Megalodon, *4*

Plankton, 9
pores, 16
predators, 12
prey, 9, 10, 16, 19, 22, *22*
pups, 20, *20*

Sand tiger shark, *24*
shortfin mako shark, 10, *10*
silky shark, *4*
size, 10
skeleton, *6*
skin, 6
smell, sense of, 16, *16*
species, 10, *20, 22*
spiny dogfish, *24*
study of, *4*, 26, *26*
swimming, 6, 9, 10, *10*, 12, *19, 26, 28*

Tail, 6, *6,*
teeth, 9, *9,* 19, *20*
tiger shark, 10, 16
tonic immobility, *28*

Whale shark, 9, *9*